First Flight

By Stephanie O'Connor

First Flight

By Stephanie O'Connor

One warm summer day, Little Butterfly wriggled and jiggled in his snug little chrysalis and wished he could get out.

He remembered when he was a little hairy caterpillar, with tiny sticky feet, gently crawling over leaves, and when he could see how beautiful the sky and all the pretty flowers were.

He didn't like being tightly wrapped up. So he wiggled and jiggled some more, desperate to see the world!

Suddenly he heard a faint little sound, and
the tiniest slit opened up in the delicate wall
of his little brown chrysalis.

Little Butterfly stopped wriggling and felt sad for a
moment. The chrysalis had been his comfy home for
days, and it seemed a pity to break it.
"But I must break it if I want to see the world," he
thought, and so he wriggled and jiggled some more
until first his head, and then his feet appeared, and he
slowly squeezed out of the little doorway, his wings
crumpled around him, excited to take his first flight.

But try as he might, Little Butterfly just couldn't fly! He tried to straighten out his wings, but they were all twisted and wet and crinkly, and they wouldn't work at all! So little Butterfly settled quietly on a leaf and waited in the sunshine all day long for his new wings to dry.

Soon it grew dark, and Little Butterfly became very tired. It had been a busy day breaking out of his chrysalis, and now he was happy to crawl under a leaf to sleep in the pale moonlight.

The next morning, Little Butterfly woke bright and early. While he had slept, his wings had dried and got big and smooth. He opened them up and quickly flew away to visit the flowers.

He flew over to the woods, and as he
flew, he saw a wonderful sight.

Beautiful flowers of all colours, orange,
yellow, pink and purple, all danced in the wind.

Their cheerful faces looked bright in the sunlight.

Little Butterfly fluttered in the sunshine. He met many other butterflies, all charming and beautiful creatures with sweeping wings who touched the flowers with a velvety softness. They were all glad to see Little Butterfly and said "Hello!" and asked if he would like to fly with them all day.

Little Butterfly said "Thank you. I will stay a little while for I like your company. But I can't stay all day because I have still so much to see today!"

The other butterflies smiled and nodded to each other, remembering their first flights when they too were little and wanted to explore.

The sky was blue and the air warm as Little Butterfly flew over river beds in valleys that cut their winding way through hills.

He fluttered in the cool blue-black shade of the orchard trees, and sheltered from summer showers

Soon it was high noon, and Little Butterfly
called to the others
"Good-bye, hope to see you tomorrow!"
and flew away for more exploring.

This time he flew near the borders of
woods and over streams and marshes,
fascinated by the murmur and gurgle of
the glistening water rushing, foaming, over
great boulders far below.

He thought about how beautiful the river
looked in the sunlight and how lucky the
flowers were to grow in such lovely places.

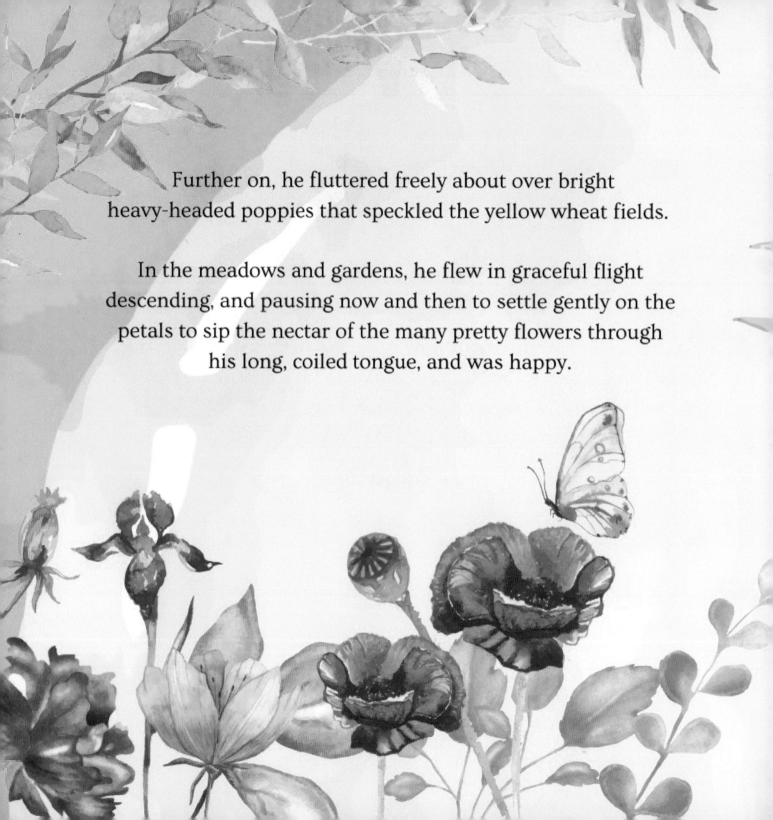

Further on, he fluttered freely about over bright
heavy-headed poppies that speckled the yellow wheat fields.

In the meadows and gardens, he flew in graceful flight
descending, and pausing now and then to settle gently on the
petals to sip the nectar of the many pretty flowers through
his long, coiled tongue, and was happy.

Sometimes Little Butterfly came to rest low
to the ground where a soft murmur of hidden
creatures rose in an invisible buzz of life.

It had been a very busy day, and Little Butterfly
had seen many things in his first flight. He especially
liked fluttering around in the sunlight and sipping sweet
nectar from the many kinds of flowers.

He had begun his day early in the morning and continued well into the evening. But as the sun started to go down, and the pretty flowers closed for the night, he selected a comfy leaf for his bed, and fluttering down, he slept until awakened the next day by the morning sunshine.

The End

Printed in Great Britain
by Amazon

19004022R00016